Charlie's Tin

By Lynda Gore

Illustrated by
Anthony Williams

FULL FLIGHT

Titles in Full Flight 8

Who Are You?	David Orme
3Dee	Danny Pearson
Doom Clone	Melanie Joyce
Too Risky!	Alison Hawes
Wanda Darkstar	Jane A C West
Galactic Games: Sci-Fi Spy Guy	Roger Hurn
Robot Eyes	Jillian Powell
Charlie's Tin	Lynda Gore
Run For Your Life	Jonny Zucker

Badger Publishing Limited
Suite G08, Business & Technology Centre
Bessemer Drive, Stevenage, Hertfordshire SG1 2DX
Telephone: 01438 791037   Fax: 01438 791036
www.badger-publishing.co.uk

Charlie's Tin ISBN 978-1-84926-470-9

Badger Publishing would like to thank Jonny Zucker for his help
in putting this series together.

Publisher: David Jamieson
Senior Editor: Danny Pearson
Design: Fiona Grant
Illustration: Anthony Williams

Contents

Chapter 1	Holiday Hell	page 5
Chapter 2	Light Fright	page 10
Chapter 3	War Zone	page 13
Chapter 4	Flying Back	page 20
Chapter 5	Getting a Name	page 24
First World War		page 30
Questions		page 32

New words:

scurrying   detector

trench   fumbled

surrounded   rations

Main characters:

Tom

Jake

Chapter 1
Holiday Hell

Tom and Jake and their parents were on a camping holiday in France.

Tom knew it would be boring without his friends. Jake was OK as brothers go but Tom always had to look after him... b.o.r.i.n.g.

But then Dad came back from the shop.

"Here you are," he said, "go and find some treasure."

"A metal detector," gasped Tom, "come on Jake, let's go!"

Tom scoured the field.

Jake scoured the field.

The metal detector finally bleeped.

Tom dug down. There was something shiny down in the hole.

He reached in but as he grabbed the small item, the earth rumbled and started to fall away to reveal a larger hole.

"Wow," whispered Jake, "that's deep."

Chapter 2
Light Fright

Tom put the small shiny tin into his pocket.

He then climbed into the hole but the sides were steep.

Tom slipped and fell with a THUMP!

"Are you OK?" he heard Jake say.

"Yes," croaked Tom. "I'm OK."

It was very dark and cold in the hole.

"Can you run back and get a torch?"
Tom shouted.

Jake raced back to the tent and returned
with a torch, which he threw down to Tom.

Tom fumbled to switch on the torch.

Suddenly a light flashed into his face, blinding him.

"WHO ARE YOU?" said a voice.

Tom nearly jumped out of his skin.

Chapter 3
War Zone

Tom could see that he was not alone.

A soldier was sitting in the trench, his uniform was different - old fashioned.

Tom could see the soldier was badly hurt.

"I will go and get help," Tom said.

He tried to climb out of the trench but he heard explosions and the rattle of machine gun fire.

"Keep your head down!" ordered the soldier, "there's a war going on."

What war? thought Tom.

"How did you find me?" asked the soldier.

Tom told the soldier about finding the tin.

"The tin was sent to me by Princess Mary," declared the soldier. "She sent all the troops a Christmas tin."

The explosions were getting louder and Tom was cold and wet.

Tom looked around the trench. There were beetles and bugs scurrying around him and the smell was making him feel sick.

Tom had to find a way out.
"I will come back with help."

Tom left the soldier.

"You must wear a gas mask," yelled the soldier.

The gas mask looked frightening but Tom put it on.

He couldn't stand up because of the enemy fire so he had to crawl on his belly through the mud.

After a while Tom saw a large wooden
crate. It read "FOOD RATIONS".

Tom opened the lid carefully.
Eyes were looking at him... "OH NO!"

Rats started jumping out of the crate.
They ran all over him.

Chapter 4
Flying Back

Tom made his way back to where the soldier was waiting.

"The rats are a big problem in the trenches," the soldier told Tom.

"They eat the food rations, and bite the soldiers while they sleep."

"This is the worst place I have ever seen," said Tom.

Suddenly there was a flash of light and a thundering sound.

Another bomb!

Tom was thrown into the air.

He was showered in mud and stones.

As the debris settled he was surrounded by darkness and then an eerie silence.

"Are you still there?" he called

But there was no answer.

Tom scrambled around in the dark.

He then heard faint voices.

"It's your regiment, they have come back for you," Tom eagerly announced.

The voices got louder.

"Tom, Tom, wake up" he heard his Mum and Dad calling.

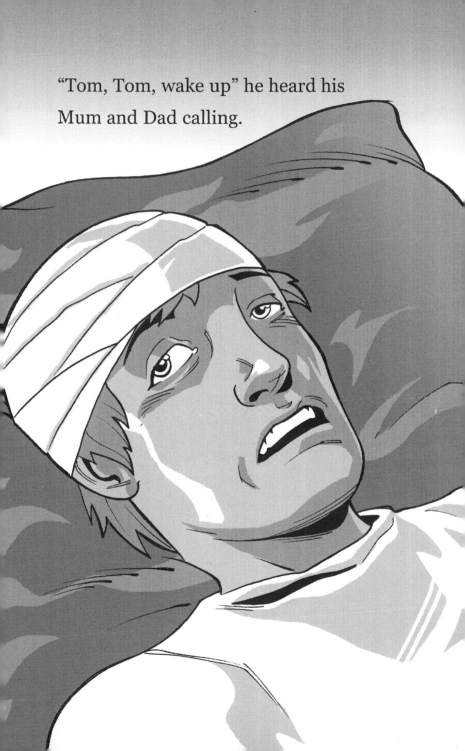

Chapter 5
Getting a Name

Tom opened his eyes. He could see his
Mum, Dad and Jake.

"Where am I?"

"You are in hospital" replied Dad.
"You fell into an old wartime trench,
and you have broken your leg."

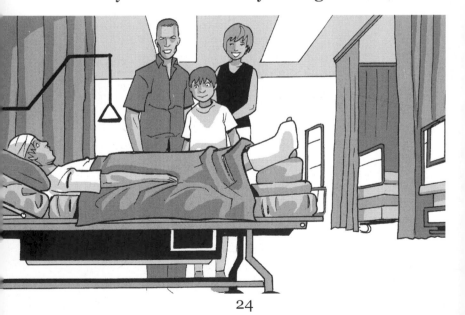

"You have been asleep for two days," sighed Jake.

Dad told Tom that the skeleton of a First World War soldier had also been found.

"The tags to identify him were missing so he will have to have an unmarked grave," said Dad.

Tom thought for a moment. He hadn't even asked the soldier his name.

The next day Tom was ready to leave hospital.

The nurse gave Tom back his muddy torn clothes that he had been wearing on the day of the accident.

"They can be thrown away," said his Mum.

"NO!" cried Tom "I need to check in the pockets."

Tom felt in the pockets and found the small tin.

The lid was engraved with the crest of Queen Mary.

Tom opened the lid and found a Christmas card, a photo, a pencil made from a bullet casing and some small pieces of metal inside.

Tom could see a printed message on the tag, "903233491 Charlie Miller".

"Look" said Tom, "This could be the soldier's name Charlie Miller."

Tom shivered as he thought about Charlie and he looked at the contents of the tin.

"This is Charlie's tin," he sniffed.

Tom was thankful that he was safe and that he had his family around him.

First World War

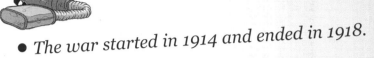

- The war started in 1914 and ended in 1918.

- Trenches were 7 feet (approx 2.2 m) deep and 475 miles (764 km) long, all dug by hand.

- All fit and healthy men aged 18 – 41 were called to war.

- Soldiers were paid 1 shilling per day (5 pence).

- Over 10 million soldiers were killed in the First World War 1914 – 1918, and half of these soldiers have no known grave.

Queen Mary Tin

- Princess Mary sent a Christmas Tin to all soldiers wearing the King's uniform and serving overseas on Christmas day 1914.

- The tins were made from brass and contained a photo, a Christmas card, a pencil and sweets or tobacco.

- A Christmas Tin was reserved for every wounded soldier and all prisoners of war.

Questions

- Where were Tom and Jake camping?

- What did their Dad buy for them?

- Who fell down the hole?

- What came out of the wooden crate?

- What was printed on the tag found in the tin?